THE LIVES WE LIVE IN HOUSES

The Lives We Live in Houses

Pauletta Hansel

Pauletta Hansel

For Jay,

My river-writing
friend

Pauletta

WIND PUBLICATIONS

International Standard Book Number 979-1-936138-40-1
Library of Congress Control Number 2011936990

First edition

Acknowledgements

My appreciation to the editors of the journals and anthologies in which these poems appear, some in previous versions:

Wind — "Day of the Dead" (The Hindman Issue, 2005)

Ohio Poetry Day Association Best of 2009 — "The Self Not Mine But Ours"

Appalachian Journal: A Regional Studies Review — "Coal" and "At Thirteen" (Volume 37, Numbers 3-4, Spring/Summer 2010)

Motif Volume Two: Come What May — "Rereading the Signs"

Penwood Review — "Falling" (Spring 2011)

Southern Women's Review — "That Winter, Fifteen" (Volume 4, Issue 4: January 2011)

Still: The Journal — "Class Lessons," Garden Sestina" and "Equinox" (5: Winter 2011)

Boomtown: Queens MFA Tenth Anniversary Celebratory Anthology Queens MFA Tenth Anniversary Celebratory Anthology — "At Thirteen"

The Mom Egg — "Shoe Shopping" (May 2011)

ABZ Journal — "Doppelganger" (Spring/Summer 2011)

For A Better World 2011: Poems and Drawings on Peace and Justice — "Coal" and "Everyday"

Motif Volume Three: Work — "Husbands" (Forthcoming)

"Day of the Dead" appeared in the chapbook *First Person*, Dos Madres Press, 2007, later reissued as a section of *What I Did There*, Dos Madres Press, 2011, which also includes "The Town" and "Why I Write." Love and thanks to Robert and Elizabeth Murphy of Dos Madres for all that they do.

Many thanks to Cathy Smith Bowers, poetry *doula* extraordinaire, and to all who have held these poems: Rebecca McClanahan, Robert Polito and all my faculty mentors, fellow students and staff at Queens MFA Program; writers in the Southern Appalachian Writers Cooperative and my Practice of Poetry and Monday Night Groups; Elizabeth Swann for use of her proofreading and other talents; Joseph Enzweiler and Richard Hague (always). I hope I've done you proud.

The cover art uses the amazing painting "Dreamscape" by John Jacob Stanley. So amazing that having seen it just once some twenty years ago, I knew I wanted it for this book. Thanks to Dave Altman in whose office the painting lives, and to Shawn Dougherty, photographer, for making its use possible. And finally, my heartfelt gratitude to Charlie Hughes for his belief in this book and his work to bring it into being.

Author photo courtesy of Elizabeth Murphy.

For my family

Contents

III. Dance Lessons

IV. The Stepmother in Fact and Fiction

V. The Self Not Mine But Ours

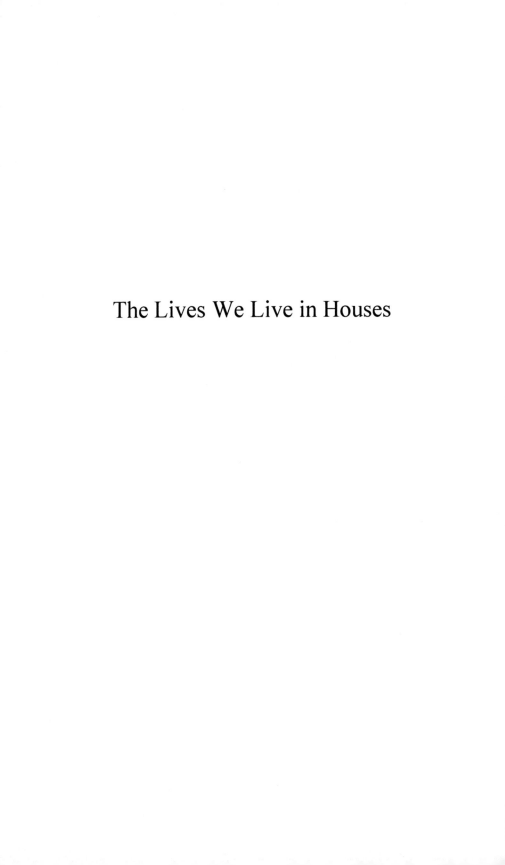

The Lives We Live in Houses

Day of the Dead

All my past loves come close now,
though their bodies live in faraway houses,
I see them, hands and faces
pressing flat against the window screens,
and I am trying to remember
why I loved them.

      This one, a beehive for a heart;
      this one who never tried
      to see inside the shroud
      I'd wrapped around my own;
      this one cracked me open,
      drank from me like honey comb;
      this one, a cliché—
      if I could make him love
      me more than whiskey or his wife
      I would be saved.

Right now the wind is blowing every
thing it can right up against another—
leaves and litter; cloud and sun.
Tree limbs scratch against tall fences;
birds huddle, feathers folded
on the wires that stretch between
the houses up and down the street,
stretch between
the ones I cannot see.

      And I am wondering
about the screens and shrouds and fences
in between the living and the dead,
about the wires held taut
between our memories

and the lives we live in houses.
I am sitting on the porch steps
listening for the silence
stretched between the passing cars,
heading home.

I

The Girl in the Photograph

Doppelganger

When she was twenty, they cut into her
and found. entwined with her heart,
her sister, tiny twin
of sinew, bits of bone and flesh.

Who among us has not wondered if
somewhere there was an other, left behind
at hospital or stolen from a crib,
living the life you would have lived,
holding your other mother's hand,
wearing your other skin?

But then to learn the other had been
with you all along—first word, first red
rust flecks on cotton panties,
the secret kiss,
hers, too.

She'd played cello, the one whose heart
had held the other. Afterwards
it hurt too much
to press against the scar.

"Where Do You Want to Spend Eternity?"

All I could imagine was an afterlife
spent in a cedar chest, only the fraying
lace of linen to amuse the hands. Death
is not sleep, they told me. So mustn't
there be endless spools of everlasting thought
filling and spilling out into the earth
below, the earth above? No rest
for the dead's restless mind.

Later the cumulus streets of heaven
had not much more appeal,
with gates that opened and closed
like the pearly clasp of Mother's purse,
letting you in, not out,
wearing the clothes they chose
for burying you, with only choir robes
for changing into should you burst a seam.

Hell hardly mattered.
I had seen beneath
the cast iron floor of Granny's cookstove,
knew there'd never be eternal life
among those burning coals.

If they had asked before they
lay me down to sleep,
I would have said,
        I'll take my heaven here—
        cool cotton sheets, with quilts
        tucked round and books,
        the ones I never mind
        to read again.

Coal

By the time I knew that coal
was something more than grit and fire
in the belly of the house
and had been held in deeper
vessels than the bucket

that once sent me sprawling
down the cellar steps
and on then to the gleaming room
where the doctor stitched
a crescent moon above my eye;

by the time that coal
was more than just the crack
in daddy's windshield, black rocks
flung from trucks careening daily
up and down our narrow road,

the coal that lined the bellies of the mountains
where our houses perched precarious
as hawks' nests or nestled in the hollowed
places at the joining of those hills
was spent.

Only the ashy seams stitched just below
the sassafras and pine, beneath
the redbud, dogwood, hickory and ferns,
under the leaf-mulched soil and sandstone
still endured.

Now that's gone too,
blasted and stripped away,
the hills a moonscape up above

the sagging houses and the towns.
The road, its hairpin

turns and crumbling berms
is gone as well;
a new highway rumbles through
the place that doctor sewed my eye:
all scars remain.

Class Lessons

I have never forgotten the little boy named Elvis
who took the seat nearest the teacher
on his first day of school, sometime in January,
after the pointy stars and Christmas trees

came down, before cut doily Valentines
and profiles of Presidential jowls. It was his birthday,
and his mother knew six years means school;
she wrapped her hair into its bun and put on

her best dress and came to town so Elvis,
with his hair slicked into place and last year's
trouser hem let down, could join us,
me and all the Susies, Davids and Toms who'd

long since seen Spot run across the printed page.
All day the teacher's frown descended;
she who'd threatened me with words
like principal and paddle when in September

I had read the year's allotment to the end.
Even her bosom grimaced when she learned
Elvis's first day by her desk
was his first at any.

Next day his seat was empty
once again; our teacher shook her head,
spoke far too sweetly of those country folk
who name their children Elvis and Loretta,

bring them to school too early—or too late.
I hold nothing else of my first year, not

the teacher's name or what I played at recess;
even my tears at being scolded for too much love

of reading are my mother's memory, not my own.
But Elvis I remember, and his mother's sin
of being country as the people
from whom I'd also come.

Visit to Cutshin Creek, 1968

Sleeping in is what we town kids do
on summer mornings—sleep until the wash
is done and toast crumbs brushed away,
and mothers take the curlers from their hair
to chat across their fences for awhile
in cotton dresses nipped in at their waists,
fathers forgotten till their tables must be set.
Sleep in, then stumble out to where the sidewalks
blind us as we ride our bikes through town
and to the cool again of friendly houses.

And so sleeping in is what I do on Cutshin Creek,
this place they've brought me to, with no
sidewalks or fences, where the reluctant sun
remains behind the hills long after morning crows.
Sleep as Granny plaits her slumbered hair
again and coils it like the snake my cousin
pulled me back from *just in time*, he said.
Sleep while the graveled voices of the men
pull from the house in pickup trucks. Sleep in
till granny's biscuits are cold and the grass
that welts my calves is almost dry and cousins
clamor at my door, amazed she's let me lie there.
Sleeping in's the only thing that is the same
as town here in the country where my mother lived,
then left, but leaves me to, come summer.

On Cutshin, even words I've learned to count on
come out wrong: my vowels too short, my consonants
too hard to pass here without notice. No matter how
I try to skirt around the men, their laughter spits
at *Larnie's girl*, plump as their hens and just about as lazy.
My cousins will not give me up so easily. Their voices

11

try to skip me safe across the slick green stones
of Cutshin Creek and up the steep bank to
the woods my mother loved. They holler down
from rocks and trees she scratched her name in.
But I live too far from this place; farther
than the sixty miles from Cutshin
to the house with shelves of books I read in soft
clipped yards on summer afternoons. And so

I sleep and then pretend to sleep some more
waiting for my parents' car to take me home.

The Town

I have been gone so long I think perhaps I have invented it, this town, but for snapshots with glimpses of place that frame the camera's clear intent. Three nuns in full habit, only the hint of forehead beneath the starched white band. Behind them steps and the wall of a church—or a school. A sidewalk where Easter patent leathers dance. A doorway where I stand, my hair in its passage from white blond to nearly black. All the rest is memory—the wall's red brick; the steep pitch of the roof above the doorway's arch; the ledge I have jumped down from, the one I walk from home to church and back again to have my picture taken in my new cloth coat and buckle shoes.

When we return, years later—my mother, my new husband and I—the town seems oddly rendered, as if captured in a globe that swirls with snow, though it is spring, the redbud barely faded, the yellow green of lawns too harsh against a sky the color of that Easter coat. Yet here it is, the place itself: the church, the school, and schoolyard too—the swings, the monkey bars, the merry-go-round, last year's grass grown up through its splintery slats and at the center where the metal pole has rusted. Forty years ago, I lay there, looking up at that same swirling sky.

Even the house we lived in, though twice we miss it, with its added wing, as my husband drives up Main Street and back again, until my mother spots the doorway, just as the photograph remembered.

At Thirteen

I decided to go barefoot,
the way another girl
that summer, '72, might tuck
a flower in her hair
or her bra away inside a drawer.
I can't remember now enough
about the self that chose that path:
maybe barefoot was a fashion
I could hide beneath
the fraying bottoms of my jeans,
or only that there were so few for me
to choose from—my hair too frizzy
to grow long and toss back
from my eyes, my legs
in mini skirt more cherub than Cher.

Even then my body urged
toward metaphor—
I longed to toughen up,
control the tears that roiled
at everything and nothing, fogging
my new glasses. Perhaps the burning
pavement underneath my soles
was salve against a deeper heat.

There was no place to go.
One street through town—
daily I walked it,
never looking up to see what they
might think of my bare feet,
the farmers and the miners
come to town, the pool hall cowboys
lounging taut against the doorways

as I passed, eyes down to guide
my feet around their pop tops
and tobacco wads, their stubs flipped
burning to the sidewalk,
their gaze
that rose to linger on the body
in which I could no longer hide.

The Girl in the Photograph

Her waist
too long
for her
body

even hidden
here beneath
a slim blue dress
that skims
her too-thin
frame

the body
she hates
not its sharp
bones
the flesh
       buttocks, breasts
small mounds that rise
to punctuate the air
around her ever-
diminishing
self.

That Winter, Fifteen

I ate mostly oranges.
First my teeth
would tear
through rind—pith,

bitter chalk
on tongue—careful
not to break too soon
the inside. Fingers

peeled away
the rest. I'd pull
apart the segments,
each to be its own

small meal, then bite
through fragile
membrane; pulp
and juice released.

> By spring my flesh
> lay light
> against my
> bones.

That was the winter
I let him tear me open.
I would have told you then
the choice was mine.

Doppelganger (2)

That summer, the last
in my parents' house,
I lived two lives—
the one in the body; the one who watched.
        I tried to see
as others did, a sideways
glimpse of girl reflected
in a shop window,
in the chrome of a father's car.
Even now I look for her,
but in that summer's photographs
there are only traces
of the girl I was, not yet the woman
I was trying hard to be.

II

Blood Line

Blood Line

It ends here,

or if not here, precisely,
in my house built of stucco and stone
the year before my father was born,

      his birthplace far from here,
      in the room behind his grandmother's kitchen,
      a tangled knot of flesh pulled from a girl
      who would not live the years
      it took to see him lengthen into boy;

if not here where, in the garden,
what small bodies I once held
against my breast are buried, claw and fur
and metal clasp of collar
beneath the peonies and lilac,

then still, it ends
with me, flesh of their flesh—

      that sad-eyed girl, now buttons and bones
      in an unmarked grave, who stares blindly
      from the single photograph of her;

      that infant whom the camera caught
      eyes closed, small hand
      a blur of motion reaching
      toward his mother's beating heart;

      and all the ones no lens recorded:
      the man who gave my father
      only seed and name, the great-grandmother

whose iron-framed bed behind the cookstove
I have conjured for my father's birth—

when I am gone, so then
is all our flesh, our blood.
Ink on a page.

My Father's Ghost

here, in the stretched shoulders
of this sweater requisitioned from his study closet
even before his death—my parents' house
that late December cold
for my blood, my father's
not yet thinned by drugs
and their diseases. Now
his bookshelves line my study walls,
my shoulders, where his shoulders were,
hunch over books
not his; he had small
use for poetry,
except for mine.
I scrawl notes along the margins
as if my hand were his.

Becoming My Mother

In dreams I wear your feet, twisted as roots,
each step a wrenching up from earth.

The morning hands that reach to smooth
the years around my eyes are more yours than mine.

When I was five, your friends would ask where
I got my curly hair, knowing I'd say,

my mother made it, as you made our
matching dresses, rickrack at the collar and the hem.

Now the skin around our collarbones is
rumpled, its fabric loose against our frames.

Boxes

My mother and I travel south to Georgetown
to get Daddy—no longer in the box
we'd left him in, wearing the suit he'd bought
for funerals. We take the road I'd driven
north to south for twenty-seven years,
my home to theirs, then back again. The last
trip north I'd made alone, hauling my parents'
moving boxes and their cat to what
we thought would be their last new home.
Today my father in his new box rests
between us. Mother and I talk of scattering
his ashes, naming the places he had loved.

Years pass, my father's box remains
beside the bed where Mother sleeps.

Later I Dream

my father is driving,
his old man shoulders hunched, and me
behind him thinking I should make him
let me take the wheel, but his car is too big—
the Lincoln, I never wanted to drive that thing.
I liked the backseat best,
my father singing
bits of songs from all his decades,
mother handing us sticks of spearmint gum.
But it's too late

for all that, the flashing lights
are coming up behind us,
the car's careening to a
stop.

Garden Sestina

Not a landscape, I told my husband, but a garden
to surround this house we newly own.
In this I am my mother's daughter.
Now the edges of our yard are never still—
always the butterflies and bees among my mother's
lilies transplanted from the edges of the home she lost.

We bought this house the year we lost
my father. There was no garden
then; the day we signed, my mother
and I planted bulbs dug from her own
yard into ours. No matter how much more I plant I still
remember the first breaking of the soil—not the daughter's

but a passing from a mother to her daughter,
beauty from the life she'd lost.
That year my mother's flowers went to seed, and still
she mourns my father first, then the garden
that she left behind. On her own
and far from what she knew, my mother

cannot live the life she loved. I know my mother
sometimes feels she has become the daughter
to the daughter; together our own
equilibrium is lost,
except here in the garden
where her wisdom still

grows up from earth. She says our town is never still;
nights she cannot sleep, my mother
hears the sirens, traffic, trains. Cut flowers from the garden
wilt in city water. This daughter

knows how much she's lost,
I mourn my own

place cradled in the crook of my own
parents' love. I once was one who had a home I still
could go to and be tended—that's lost
too for me in ways my mother
and I never speak of in this city where the daughter
tends those things uprooted from her mother's garden.

The Ginkgo Tree

I plant outside my study window,
his favorite tree, the way
it drops all leaves at once
in its gold glory.
While he lived it was the maple
I loved best, its last leaf
falling red
in late December snow.

Why I am Grateful for Dreams

Turning to walk into my friend's
sturdy embrace, I enter the frail circle
of my father's arms and let him hold me,
knowing he is dead, believing too his birch bark
cheek against my own.

My white cat blinks his eye
to call me to his favorite chair
and I am dropping books and bags,
rushing to his familiar fur before he is
again old bones beneath the lilac.

Longing

These words today, as though
from dream: *My father*
never lost his longing.
And it's true—there could
never be enough—no, try again—
My father lived his life
as if there could someday be plenty,
but maybe not for him.

The third winter now without him,
my mind makes such pronouncements.
Asleep, I read aloud from Sanskrit:
The year my father met his oracle was 1963.
Awake, I ponder with my mother—
1963. My brother born.
John Kennedy dies.
The year he met Merton?

She cannot tell me either, though she thinks
of nothing but him still—All stories lead to Daddy.
I have begun to test this theory: Can she pull him
from a flannel shirt, a broken lock,
the feeble arc of winter sun?
My mother, in the lasting wake
of my father's death,
takes on his longing, wears it
as I wear his stretched out sweater,
roll up his sleeves,
claim his ink stains as my own.

Buried

Because I cannot bear to think of him,
my mother's cat, yesterday warm
fur under my hand, now in the ground
beneath the cherry tree,
his body softening in spring rain,

I busy myself with prettying his grave.
We buried him in our yard,
not in hers—she said she had too many
hard things, roots and rocks. Because
I cannot stand here and remember

Mother's tears at one more death,
knowing all death holds my father's,
all loss the loss of him, I think instead
of strangers in my garden, years from now,
digging up these irises

that mark her old cat's grave
to plant another lilac or a cherry,
finding a jawbone and the buckle of a collar
as they replace the old growth
we leave behind.

Falling

I.

My mother, at the threshold
of her house, falls back
as if the world outside her door
has slammed it shut,
as if the trees, the birds,
the roses she planted and pruned
have all said no to her.

That isn't why she falls.
There are words the doctors say
to tell us why her legs will not
step up, then down
across that rise of wood,
the doorsill.

My mother says, *as if a hand
has pushed itself against my knees.*
I say, my mother's at a threshold;
we do not know what ground
is there to greet her.

II.

My mother, walking, does not walk alone.
This is not Bible verse—
there are two walkers, neither of them her:
the metal quadruped to hold her as she crosses
sills and curbs I never knew were there;
the one with wheels for level ground.
There is a cane to move from room to room,
chair backs and tabletops to lean on
as she stands. And me,
my eyes held steady on her legs
to will their bending up and straightening down:
Don't fall, don't fall,
my muttered mantra.

33

III

Dance Lessons

Pronouns

Ever since the year
my father died
I have been trying to write
a poem about pronouns

how my mother moved that year
from *we* to *I*
and I at 47, newly married
became *we*

      In this house too big for me alone,
      my silver clanks against my dinner plate

          my husband, at work two time zones
          west of here, loosens his tie

          a few blocks south
          my mother dozes in my father's chair

I phone:
    Won't you eat tonight at my house?
    We'll just stay home, she says.

Husbands

My mother likes a man who works. She likes
my husband's muddy knees, grass stains on the cuffs.
She loved my father, though when weekends came
he'd sleep till nine and would not lift
his eyes up from the page to move the feet
she'd vacuum under. On Saturdays my husband
digs the holes for her new roses,
softening the clay with peat and compost.
He changes bulbs she can no longer reach
and understands the inside of her toaster.
My father's feet would carry him from chair
to bookshelf, back again till Monday came.
My mother likes to tell my husband
sit down in this chair and put your feet up.

Dance Lessons

We should get out more, I say, so we go out
dancing. In the storefront studio, we foxtrot and waltz
in place. Our instructor shows how changing

directions is like a three-point turn, backing the car
into a driveway, pulling out again. He knows
his audience: we are mostly

Fords and Chevrolets tonight— I'm talking
early models, definitely pre-disco, the ones
with window cranks, that fishtail in the snow.

There is snow tonight, way too much of it, piled
above our heads in the corners of the parking lot.
Maybe twenty of us made it here, a Nissan

or two mixed in among us rear-wheel drives.
At least we're not the oldest ones; I'm guessing
those guys still play eight-tracks. My husband says it's

easier without the music, just remembering
the steps, not following the song. It's hard
not to compare—the way that couple glides, another

tries a twirl we haven't even learned.
When the music stops, we are
the only ones still dancing.

Ghazal

Before we met a longing had been wrung from me:
worn garment, twisted nearly dry, I stood before you.

You never knew I almost turned from you, my love
still clinging to the heels of him before you.

A girl turned woman clutching the shape that absence made;
I thought all love was fueled by loss before you.

We say *I love you* each good-bye, my sleep-filled mouth
too slow for the refrain, *I love you more,* before you.

I've heard each human pair contains a lover and belovèd;
I knew which one Pauletta was but for you.

Valentine's Day

My mother hands me
a love letter
my father wrote the year
I was born—*you may want to*

write about it, she says.
My husband gives me
chocolate and new tires
for my car. I try to write

him a love poem; it cannot find
its shape. My father had no fear
of sentiment or symbol;
on the knees of his heart he

thanked my mother for their *most holy*
human love and she kept it folded
safe for fifty years through
moves and floods and death.

Don't lose it, she tells me.

Rereading the Signs

I once believed that as my ancestors
smelled snow before it came or,
ears to ground, heard buffalo,
I, too could sense the seismic shifting of my fate.
Maybe I heard too often how my parents'
love was at first sight.
I thought my future would leave bread crumbs.

      My parents' story: first him, all limbs
      and spectacles, poor boy on campus
      kitchen duty, bored with scooping ice cream
      from the carton to the bowl,
      rinsing the scoop and then again.
      She enters now, as if in spotlight, all else fades;
      he drops the ice cream into the rinse water not once,
      not twice (how many, Daddy?!) and tells his friend,
      She's the girl I'll marry.

But though I do remember April 1992,
branches thick with blossoms
beneath spring's impossible snow,
nothing in me quickened,
no restless turning in my dreams
as my someday, almost-daughter was born.

Twelve years past the snowy April of his daughter's birth,
my not-yet-husband and I each placed a singles ad,
more like ordering Chinese than reading tea leaves.
We tell the story of how we, in our twenties
could have met, how we frequented the same bars,
had friends who knew us both,
just not together.

I like to think he was the one
I seem now to recall:
that crowded barroom, smoke in my eyes.

The Long View

We took to kissing
at overlooks, those early courtship days.
We'd drive away from town and find new
trails for walking, never the same ridge twice.

December seems an odd month
for such pastoral wooing. A few leaves
clung to branches. The sky always gunmetal grey.
The caw of crows. The empty milkweed pods.
The burrs catching on our sleeves.

You'd walk ahead, or I would, wrapped
in winter coats and the worn habits
of our solitude. But then—blessed geography—
the curvature of earth, the world laid out before us...

It was months before you told me you feared heights.
By then it didn't matter that our rite was born in part
by your desire to pull me from the edge of danger.
Even now I will not make too much of this,
thankful for whatever paths that brought us
to that sudden opening of view.

Then

There was a certain melancholy
at dusk, a curtain slowly drawn,
its restless specks of dust let loose
to catch the downward
slant of sun, then settle once again
into the heavy folds of night.

Or this, at least, is how I see it now,
my single life: years—decades—
of watching from my window
lights in one house, then another,
flickering on from room to room,
returning to my desk or page-strewn bed
to write.

I'd not go back
to that single lamp light on my page,
but sometimes now at dusk
I'll slip out from my own house, bright
through all its windows, and let
the darkening sky rest in me for awhile,
remembering the nights shot through
with longing, fiery sweet, a meteor
burning lonely in descent.

Tonight the Gibbous Moon

becoming or becoming not
round and full and
perfect silver as an
unplucked plum.
The almost moon
or almost
not.

And me tonight, not
mother, maid, nor crone;
the moon's pull waning—
this month maybe
the downward
ache, the meager egg
or maybe
not.

Love Poem, Upon Turning Fifty

Even at forty I could not have imagined you and the daily
breathing in and out of marriage, sometimes in unison, sometimes
in syncopated no-rhythm-at-all, sometimes the pant of labor or
lust, but always your breath on the back of my neck as I sleep, and
your hand reaching round to my waiting hand, and I could not
have imagined a love poem without longing.

So much longing. So much want and need and doing without. I
apologize now to myself at fifteen and thirty and even at forty for
all that hunger come to naught, or not to what I thought would
come to be. I've come to plenty, really, plenty of flesh on my
bones; everything is just so comfortable rubbing up against
everything else, thigh to thigh and breast to ribcage and your belly
resting above my butt as we sleep; your breath, my breath,
breathing not as one but as a pair of us. And me, rising to trip over
that pair of your shoes flung akimbo....I could not have imagined
a love poem with shoes.

IV

The Stepmother in Fact and Fiction

Shoe Shopping

She has come back from camp
a vegan and now we must
buy Birkenstocks, though she still teeters—
Will people think they're ugly? she asks,
as if I might know.

Last year it was spike heels
to match the wrong prom dress
I'd helped her choose: missing the mark
of *almost like the other girls', but different.*
I cannot help

but think about another pair
of slippers now, though I'm the wrong mother
for such gifts in that story, too, step-
ping beside her in my sturdy shoes,
neither the earthly one nor the divine.

Loving the Daughter

was easy, like when I learned
to read at four or five,
cracked the code
on the detergent box and
ALL
was in mind's reach.
By the time I knew that words
were tricky,
could turn on you
mid-syllable,
I was already hooked.

Prosody

At sixteen my stepdaughter writes only
in iambic pentameter. No substitutions allowed.

"What's the big deal about Shakespeare,"
she tells me. "His iambic sucks; it doesn't even scan."

> My friends with daughters talk of how those bodies
> once as close as limbs or breasts now dress behind
> closed bedroom doors and suffer hugs around
> their shoulders only, all angles and planes.

I think of Sarah's poetry at thirteen, my earliest and only access,
my praise the closest to a mother's arms she would allow.

"I was so emo then," she says; now she will *tell all the truth*
        but tell it slant—
but "no slant rhyme, that sucks as much as Shakespeare's
        lesser sonnets."

Sarah: her name itself a variation from that pattern
she tells me she insists upon in poems she never shows me.

On Moist

my stepdaughter's
"most hated word,"
but she tells me this while,
radio quiz show on, we wait
in the idling car for her father,
and *moist* is the answer
to *what is the most hated word*,
so I do not quite believe her.

I suppose she is thinking about
the insides of things.
A wound. A cat's rough tongue
against an unprepared chin. The pink
around an eye reminding us
we're as much water as bone.

Or maybe at seventeen
her mind strays
farther down.

I do not press her for a reason.

Her father will not
do the laundry when she visits;
he will not reach his hand
into the cavernous damp
and pull thongs and C-cups
into light.

These are his rules;
I let them be.

Loving the Son

Maybe if I'd held the bundle of your body,
your hand across a busy street,
if by the year we met you had not been

a son suspended there between magnetic poles,
pulled and dropped
and pulled again away from the other.

Now you are the phone call to my husband in the night,
a disembodied voice
disturbing dream. Now you seem suspended still—boy

lost inside the man you are becoming.

Loving the Mother

might be like teaching myself to love
the fairytale witch; I would really have to
think about it, fill in the back-story
no one wanted to write
          ignore the wheedling voice
          the grasping hands
but couldn't that be any mother,
even mine,
or me, depending on who
tells the tale?

The Stepmother in Fact and Fiction:
A Poetic Survey

I.

There is no mirror
like a daughter.
I read those old tales
differently now: the queen
displaced from her own story,
stepping from ever-happy bride
to minor plot line in a single page.
The world belongs
to daughters and to sons.
I never knew this, having none,
but rather saw myself the hero
or the heroine; neither age nor gender
mattered in the reading of myself
into the quest. Now the text
would have me sit
and watch, a bit of knitting
or a cauldron
at my twisted feet.
No daughter is a mirror, either;
there's the rub—no matter
how a mother polishes
the glittery surface of her vanity,
the girl remains the girl.

II.

Far too many mothers
in these tales—the ones who die
in childbirth, their destinies fulfilled;
foolish wives, trading
their daughters for a snack;

rich ones whose curfews
have a girl come scurrying
home before the music's ended;
mothers who send children
from the table with gristle and bone;
the ones who'd rather gnaw
a daughter's bones
than feed her even that.
This girl of mine will claim
no mother as her own.
She casts her story line back further;
she would spring fully loaded
from her father's head.

III.

What then of the fathers?
There are three sorts, like wishes
or brave deeds, improbable at best:
one turns his back and wrings
his kingly hands (poor girl, poor me!);
another lingers just outside the story;
the third one has no better knack
at picking daughters' husbands
than his wives.
They are the same father
in the end—blessings bestowed,
the daughter's love restored—
for fathers do not have to die
to let a girl close one book,
open another.

IV.

A stepmother's more like a mirror,
fated to watch another's tale unfold.
My new daughter at thirteen

had long since chosen
her foe. Her mother
was the one to play the role
assigned in other stories
to those like me, come-lately.
Their village was not big enough
for yet another wicked queen.
A stepmother can be neither,
not the womb to which the girl
refuses to return, nor the ladder
she will climb triumphant
as she leaves
this story behind.

V

The Self Not Mine But Ours

Why I Write

Always the hope
it is more artichoke than onion,
and I am heading toward
a plump, sweet mystery
the surface never can reveal.

Or like tapping mother's crystal goblets,
each resonating note heard only
in relation to the other—
yes this; not that; these together
make the tune.

February Fugue

I.

One gray morning follows
yesterday's reprieve
and I have already forgotten
how to be grateful.
Somewhere outside my house
workmen drill and drill
as if to pry gloom
from the center of February,
but they will not succeed.
I am sullen, yes,
and this poem is too; we have
forgotten how else we might be.

II.

February dreams are *Coyote*,
the Trickster, howling
his desolate song.
This morning I wake
to your breathing back;
I had even forgotten you.

III.

After the thaw,
mud.

IV.

Already the branches
of redbud
thicken at their tips;
they will not forget
how to bloom.

The Self Not Mine But Ours

There were so many ways then to forget my
self—tumbling, rolling down green hill,
my arms held tight against my body,
a gentle push and I was
only air and earth, earth and air
until I landed soft into self again.

Or swinging round and round, feet in air,
my arms held by a child just larger
than myself, then suddenly released
to freeze into whatever
shape I found, no longer me:
dizzy, breathing statue.

And how, when disappearing into sleep,
I would spiral to a distant point,
dissolving into no one and everything,
then startled from that place
before sleep came, the grief to find
myself alone inside my body.

Equinox

Our bones are cold
inside the moist caves
of our flesh. We stand blinking
on our door stoops,
sniffing the air like beasts
we still remember how to be.
Around the edge of stubborn snow
rises a whiff of last year's garden,
stalk and leaf and fruit
nipped black, then frozen,
rotting back into the earth.
Above, smudged branches
brush restlessly against a tepid sky.

Green is pressing up
through bulb and mud and leaf mulch
like breath that rises through our bodies
and returns.

Waiting in Spring

This morning I sit by the window and wait
for the poem that is not coming.
High in the wild
cherry tree the caterpillars hover;
beyond blooming of tulip and redbud,
magnolia and pear
they will fall on our pale
pink necks as we till the soil
of the garden that was and will be.

Perhaps I should go down
into the clay and humus of yesterday's work
where I laid, brick-by-brick,
a border,
arbitrary divide for all that waits
for what in seed or root
is always underneath.

How To Write A Poem

If summer, you might risk a walk outside to see what's bloomed in the night. Today, my dahlias swoon against the fading daisies. The sunflower, already tall as last year's plant that bent its shaggy head and shook down seeds, has set its bud.

Don't stop to prune the ragged edge, the withered shoot; there'll be other days for clippers and shears.

Did you hope for more instruction? We could go back, prepare the soil, cut limbs that block the sun, weed out invasive settlers.

Now's not the time. Let rise whatever's dropped down and taken root.

Always Looking At the Wrong Thing

Not the sweet bruised flesh
but the worm's sharp wounding.

Not the fruit
but its weight.

Not the day
but the dark that frames it.

Not the garden
but the gate.

The Garden, Late Fall

We tire of them at last: the dahlias and cosmos,
the roses, budding still on spindly stems
no thicker than their thorns.

The light turns from our yards
as we would now but for
these oddly blooming few

in the decaying rubble of our gardens.
We pray for frost—too soon for snow,
but far too late for gathering rosebuds.

The scent of summer clings
to dampened soil; we long to turn
it under, let the living nestle down

beneath the leaf mulch as we, inside our houses,
turn on lamps against November,
wait again for spring.

Notes

The Self Not Mine But Ours is a line from *Poetics* by A. R. Ammons

Always Looking At the Wrong Thing takes its title from a line by Molly McEvilley, and borrows its form from Dorianne Laux's *What Would You Give Up.*

About the Author

Pauletta Hansel's previous collections of poetry include *Divining* (WovenWord Press, 2002), *First Person* (Dos Madres Press, 2007) and *What I Did There* (Dos Madres Press, 2011). She received her MFA from Queens University of Charlotte in 2011. A native of eastern Kentucky and a graduate of Antioch College/Appalachia, Pauletta was involved in establishing early networks of Appalachian writers, including West Virginia's Soupbean Poets and the Southern Appalachian Writers Cooperative. She is a current editor of *Pine Mountain Sand and Gravel*, SAWC's literary publication, and leads various poetry and other programs in and around Cincinnati, where she's lived since 1979.

CPSIA information can be obtained at www.ICGtesting.com
Printed in the USA
LVOW13s1206221013

358025LV00001B/28/P